THE TOP PERFORMER'S GUIDE TO SPEECHES
AND PRESENTATIONS

*Essential Skills That
Put You On Top*

TIM URSINY, PhD &
GARY DeMOSS
WITH JIM MOREL

SOURCEBOOKS, INC.
NAPERVILLE, ILLINOIS

Published by Sourcebooks, Inc.
P.O. Box 4410, Naperville, Illinois 60567-4410
(630) 961-3900
Fax: (630) 961-2168
www.sourcebooks.com

Library of Congress Cataloging-in-Publication Data

Ursiny, Timothy E.
 The top performer's guide to speeches and presentations / Tim Ursiny & Gary
DeMoss, with Jim Morel.
  p. cm.
 Includes bibliographical references and index.
 ISBN 978-1-4022-0775-4 (hardcover : alk. paper) 1. Public speaking. 2. Business
presentations. I. DeMoss, Gary. II. Morel, Jim. III. Title.

PN4129.15.U77 2007
651.7'3--dc22

                                  2007019321

Printed and bound in the United States of America.
BG 10 9 8 7 6 5 4 3 2 1

DEDICATION

From Tim:
To my father, Kenneth Richard Ursiny; he gave the best
fifteen-minute sermons of any preacher I have ever heard.

From Gary:
To my ultimate speaking role model Barry Asmus and to
all the great speakers at VanKampen.

From Jim:
To my children Tom, Kaleen, and Marques.

ACKNOWLEDGMENTS

When you have done a series of books with a publisher you get to know them very well. Dominique Raccah and the talented team at Sourcebooks never fail to support and guide us. We are indebted to each of them, especially Peter Lynch and Erin Nevius. Along with the editorial team, we'd like to thank the incredible sales and PR teams at Sourcebooks for their constant support.

We thank our families for having patience with our laptops that are always out, and for putting up with our many road trips.

We thank our clients and our audiences, who challenge us to become better each and every year.

Thanks to the many speakers who shared their wisdom with us. Their names and contributions can be found throughout this book.

TABLE OF CONTENTS

INTRODUCTION

DEVELOPING YOUR PERSONAL SIGNATURE AS A SPEAKER

Have you ever wanted to jump into a time machine and redo a presentation? Most of us would love another chance at one of our talks. In fact, the pastor of my church would love to go back in time to redo his first sermon. He shared with me how he felt the first time he was at the pulpit. Pastor Kelly is a confident man, and he initially felt great about his preaching premiere. He had prepared well, studied his passages, practiced in front of the mirror, and he was ready to inspire and motivate the congregation. The actual sermon went well. He emphasized his words in all of the right places, he spoke with conviction and passion, and, in general, he felt like he imparted a message of impact and value. After the sermon, parishioners were kind with their comments and he went to the restroom feeling positive and hopeful about his career as a minister. In the bathroom he noticed one thing that he had forgotten to do before his presentation: Pastor Kelly had forgotten to zip up his pants. Amazingly, as we interviewed scores of great speakers for this book, we found that leaving one's fly down was the most common blunder. So if you just remember to zip up you will be ahead of the crowd!

Our point is that there are many things that can go wrong in a presentation, but by learning a disciplined way to build your personal signature as a speaker you can minimize mistakes and maximize your chances at "wowing" the crowd. Everyone has to exercise discipline and preparation, but you also have to add the character that makes a speech distinctly your own.

Why Top Performers Must Be Great at Presentations

Anyone who has to do any form of public speaking can benefit from learning what top performers know about presentations. Imagine that you are about to stand up in front of your boss and team and try to sell your concept to the entire group. The stakes are high and the pressure is immense. Are you up to the task?

Few things terrify people as much as public presentations. Speaking before a team, a rotary club, a large audience, giving a toast at a wedding—almost all of us face this fear of public speaking in one form or another in our lives. Your ability to present well can impact your career and personal branding in an extremely positive way. You can be a great performer in all other areas of your work, but giving a lousy presentation can cause your brand to plummet. Conversely, you could be an average performer and give a drop-dead presentation and your personal branding can go through the roof. Your public persona reveals you as confident or unconfident, competent or incompetent; it reveals to all those watching just how good you are. Your branding is at stake and failing to prepare could cost you heavily.

Who Is This Book For?

Anyone who has to make public presentations can benefit from this book. This includes:

- Professional speakers
- Managers and executives
- Sales professionals who present to clients and prospects
- Pastors and teachers
- Really, anyone who is asked to speak in a public setting (giving toasts, speaking in a team meeting, etc.)

Whether you are speaking to large audiences or presenting to one person, these principles always apply. Therefore, whether you are selling to a prospect, giving a meaningful toast at your boss's retirement party, speaking before the board of directors, or presenting your findings in a team meeting, this book can help you give a drop-dead presentation.

The Core Concept: Using Your Whole Mind

The main concept of *The Top Performer's Guide to Speeches and Presentations* is the idea of being a "whole brain speaker." Most books on speaking only address the left side of the brain; they focus on the structure of your talk and the information that you are going to convey. We know from studying top performers that this is only half of the battle of mastering presentation skills—top presenters are also able to address the right side of the brain. In other words, all top presenters connect with their audience emotionally. And what is the primary way that speakers connect emotionally with their audiences? Their stories—experiences they've had that everyone can relate to. And the more genuine and personal the story the better. This emotional connection will make your audience not just *think* about what you said, but will actually move them to action.

So later in this book we will help you build personal stories which will connect with the audience. You don't want people to just *think* about what you said; you want them to be moved by your presentation; moved emotionally and moved to action.

Humans are wired to connect more through emotions than through information. Research shows that we have emotional responses almost always before we have a logical response, and a wise speaker knows to tap into this. It is like walking into a professional office that has a strong receptionist acting as the gatekeeper. If you offend the receptionist, you may be left in that waiting area for a *very* long time. If the receptionist likes you, you may be ushered in right away to see the CEO. In this analogy the receptionist is the right side of the brain, which mainly recognizes emotions over logic. If the right brain gets it and is impressed, the information is more likely to get to the left side of the brain (the CEO).

After studying top speakers around the world, training thousands of people in presentation skills, and diagnosing what makes some speakers fail and others soar, we have come to this conclusion: Top presenters know how to impact both sides of the brain in a powerful and moving way. Despite this, most training in presentation skills focuses on left-brain activities. This leaves it up to each individual speaker to accidentally discover the power of addressing both sides of the brain on their own. We want you to learn to connect with your audience intentionally and effectively. This means developing your personal signature as a speaker. In other words, we want you to develop your own style and branding. You want a signature that represents you at your very best. With the proven exercises and advice in this book, you can develop a personal signature that will make your presentations and reputation soar.

Objectives and Overview

If you read this book and do each of the exercises, you WILL take your presentation ability to the next level. We are going to help you by addressing both style and structure, the two things needed to develop your personal signature as a speaker. We will aid you in becoming a motivating speaker rather than someone who simply relays information. We will address common presentation blunders and how to avoid them. By the end of this experience, you will have a huge jump-start on developing your own personalized speaking style. And just like a powerful talk, this book has both structure and style. Each chapter features the following sections:

- **Have you ever**—Each chapter will start with a story or illustration related to the chapter topic. (For the sake of simplicity, we will use "I" when telling stories without identifying which author is technically speaking.)

- **What top performers know about presentations**— In this section we will share the strategies practiced by top performers that take their presentation ability to the next level.

- **Tips from the pros**—We interviewed speaking professionals and top presenters to gather experiences and insights related to fears, preparation, and tactics for successful public speaking. In this section we will introduce you to some great presenters and have them answer the following questions:

  1. What was your greatest fear starting out as a speaker?
  2. What was your worst speaking blunder?

3. How do you prepare for a talk?
4. What distinguishes you as a speaker?
5. What is the #1 most important thing you can do to make a talk soar?

Taking your speaking to the next level—Each chapter ends with exercises that will strengthen your presentation skills. To fully benefit from this book, it is crucial that you do these exercises.

Read on to discover your personal signature and build your brand as a superstar presenter!

SECTION I

THE
ESSENTIALS

CHAPTER 1

STYLE AND STRUCTURE

Have You Ever…?

Have you ever spent a lot of money on something that you ended up not using? Let me tell you about a gentleman I once knew who had extreme buyer's remorse. I was attending a major event for leaders across the country. At this particular event, each speaker paid $10,000 for the opportunity to stand up for five minutes in front of this elite group of professionals. This was their chance to speak to a group of influential buyers who they usually would have no chance to get in front of. So the cost was significant, the stakes were high, and the ability to present well was crucial.

Unfortunately, the first speaker got up and was obviously nervous. He was stumbling over his words and ended up thanking the audience for about one minute (20 percent of his allotted presentation time). At this point I was no longer looking at him—I was looking at the audience. Often when we study speakers, the best way to gauge their ability is looking at the audience because the people listening will tell you everything you need to know. As I watched I noticed that a third of the crowd was fiddling with their pens or looking around. The speaker then went on to give detailed information about his credentials and experience for about two minutes (40 percent of his presentation time). At this point about half of the audience was engrossed in some other activity, such as chatting with their neighbors. Three minutes into his five-minute presentation he finally started to talk a little about his product, but did so by dumping as much information as possible into that last two minutes. By the end of this presentation, no one cared about anything he had to say. Ten thousand dollars were down the drain because he did not know how to engage his audience.

In contrast, the next speaker got up and told a short but engaging story about himself and how he worked with clients. He told the audience that he had three points to make and then he made them concisely, sharing just enough information for the audience to understand. He ended by specifically requesting that his audience buy his product. I looked around and saw 125 sets of eyes completely on him and connected to his message. His investment of $10,000 was well spent. The point? When you get your moment to shine, don't waste it! Use that moment to impact others and take your brand to the next level.

What Top Performers Know about Presentations
One Shining Moment

The very last thing they do at the end of the NCAA Tournament is play the anthem *One Shining Moment*.

Eyes well up with tears as this powerful song accompanies a highlight reel of the most outstanding plays of the tournament. It is a video of the best of the best—the plays that stand above all the others. But you don't have to play basketball in order to get your chance for a shining moment. Everyone reading this will have that chance. In that moment, all eyes will be on you. Are you ready? How well will you shine when the pressure is on? Maybe you have already had one chance at this moment. How did you do? This book is about making you better in that one shining moment.

"You'll never get another chance to make a first impression" is a clichéd expression that happens to be very true, and especially so when you are in front of an audience. These are times when you only get one chance to shine, to brand yourself and impact others. Think of the sales professional who gets five minutes in front of a hot prospect, the executive who has just a few minutes to MC a corporate event, the worker who presents to upper management attempting to get approval for a much-needed budget increase, or the keynote speaker who has to motivate and inspire an audience before the big corporate event. These moments offer one shining chance to:

- Raise your brand
- Demonstrate your expertise
- Turn one opportunity into multiple opportunities

Conversely, if you do not know how to handle that moment you can also:

- Destroy your credibility
- Exhibit your insecurity
- Get blacklisted from greater opportunities

This is why it is so crucial to know how top performers handle presentations—there is much on the line, and top performers know how to shine in that moment.

Style and Structure

As we've said, if you know the substance of your talk the two key components of a successful presentation are structure and style. Our objective is to help you master both of these in order to build your personal signature as a speaker. And you know the value of a signature, right? A signature is very difficult to forge because it is uniquely yours. By working from a solid structure and tapping into your personal style, you can build a signature as a speaker that no one else can replicate.

Behind every great presentation is a solid structure or format. Great speakers do not fly by the seat of their pants: They take time to research, form, and test the structure of their presentation. After determining the structure, they focus their attention on the style of presenting. Your style is how you deliver your message. What creates your presence in front of the team, on stage, or presenting to that prospect? It is the use of your eyes, voice, and body. Style is how you share your stories and the way you move in the room. You are not just giving out information and you are not just being funny—you are creating an opportunity for change and growth.

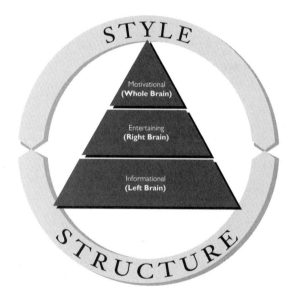

Three Main Levels of Speakers

Style and structure go hand in hand, and a presentation missing either one of them is a presentation that will fail. There are three main levels of speakers, and your mastery over both style and structure will determine to which level you will rise.

Informational Speakers

Informational speakers are very good at just that: getting out information. They usually do well with the structure portion of the presentation, but they lack style. In other words, they do well as left-brain speakers but ignore the power of addressing the right side of the brain. You can generally spot an informational speaker by the following signs:

1. They have lots of PowerPoint slides, usually with many charts and graphs.
2. Their visual aids have way too much text.
3. They don't tell stories.
4. They repeat the information that you see on their slides.
5. They are very dependent on their slides or notes and are lost without them.

Again, they may be excellent at relaying information and can be very bright people, but they usually fail to engage their audience so their wisdom is lost on an audience who can't follow along or lose interest.

Entertaining Speakers

Some people are able to move up to become entertaining speakers. Speakers at this second level focus on the right side of the brain: Great entertaining speakers have mastered style and their delivery is funny and entertaining. They engage their audience with humor, anecdotes, or stories and are able to keep listeners interested in what they're saying. People will walk out of the presentation saying things like:

- *That was interesting*
- *He was funny*
- *She had a lot of energy*

To be an entertaining and engaging speaker you do not necessarily have to tell funny jokes. However, you do need to know how to keep peoples' attention while sharing some information. The only thing that entertaining speakers often fail to do is truly inspire and impact the audience. The presentation was a nice experience, but leads to nothing else. While an entertaining speaker may be great on style, he or she may lack the structure to truly share information in a way that leads to action.

Motivational Speakers

All great speakers and presenters motivate people to change their behavior. Now, when we say "motivational speaker" we are not necessarily talking about the rah-rah dramatists in infomercials on late night television. What we are talking about is having the ability to impact others. As a presenter or speaker, do you have the ability to motivate people to action? When someone hears you present, do they change their mind? Do they want to do something about what you have said? Do they buy what you are selling? These are all aspects of a powerful motivational speech.

If motivating, convincing, and persuading are part of your career, you need to become a motivational speaker. Engage the whole brain of your audience: entice the left-brain with solid and reliable information that is well-structured and in a logical sequence, and address the right side of the brain with entertaining and meaningful stories, examples, and anecdotes. Entertain them to keep their attention and use compelling facts and figures to sway them to your viewpoint.

The result is that people walk away from your presentation with a change in their perspective and, thus, a change in their behavior. Information is just information, and level-one speakers will present that information in a dull and uninteresting fashion that ensures their audience won't listen. You can be entertaining and funny, but second-level speakers will have people leaving the presentation wondering what they learned. You want to become the motivating speaker who taps into the whole brain. When this individual walks off stage, the audience says, "He is incredible; we want him back and we need to do what he suggested." In other words, they are not just saying it was a great presentation, but that you were a great presenter. Your brand goes up and people want to hear you speak again—no matter what the topic! That is the level we all want to achieve. That is the level of the whole brain speaker who has mastered both style and structure, bringing the two together in an inspiring combination.

The speaker who has mastered structure without style is our informational speaker. He is intelligent, capable, and knowledgeable, but will bore his audience to death. In contrast, the entertaining speaker has mastered style. He knows how to talk to his audience, but without structure his presentation can come off as lacking content. If you do not want to be seen as boring or fluffy, combine structure with style to become that speaker who motivates people to change their behavior. This level of speaker truly cares about impact and confidently presents his or her message.

The Speaking Drug: Adrenaline

Regardless, whether novice or pro, nervousness before a presentation is normal and to be expected. If you have played competitive sports, think about your most important game. How did you feel in the moments before it began? You were likely nervous, tense, and a little wired. Think about your biggest speaking event up to this point—how did your body feel? You probably felt about the same: nervous, tense, and a little wired. The reason you felt that way before the big game or before making a presentation is adrenaline. Athletes know the value and power of a good level of adrenaline, and great speakers should know the same thing. Doing a presentation without adrenaline means that you won't put in the energy or effort needed to knock the ball out of the park. A little adrenaline keeps us on our toes and causes us to spend time perfecting our presentation. However, too much adrenaline is a disaster and can turn a potentially good presentation into a humiliating experience.

In psychology, the effect of anxiety on performance is classically measured on a curve. Basically, there is an amount of anxiety that is good for performance. When you're at this peak, you will structure and deliver your presentation with enthusiasm and energy. However, as your anxiety increases your performance will decrease. You might speak too quickly, stumble over words, appear self-conscious as you present, etc. This is a high level of damaging fear.

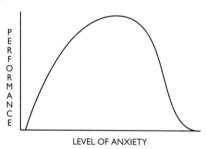

LEVEL OF ANXIETY

Fortunately, if you follow our suggestions for structuring your presentation and developing your own personal signature as a speaker, you will be able to keep your anxiety at a productive level. Out-of-control adrenaline can be a major contributing factor to many presentation mistakes.

Common Presentation Blunders

Think of the last time you saw someone fail at a presentation. It is very difficult to watch (and distressingly easy to do)! Carmine Gallom, author of *10 Simple Secrets of the World's Greatest Business Communicators*, offers these common speaker mistakes:

1. Reading from notes
2. Avoiding eye contact
3. Dressing down
4. Fidgeting, jiggling, and swaying
5. Failure to rehearse
6. Standing at attention (i.e., too rigidly)
7. Reciting bullet points from your PowerPoint
8. Speaking too long
9. Failing to excite your audience
10. Ending with an inspiration deficit

Throughout this book, we will cover ways to conquer these common errors as well as damaging habits such as:

a. Lacking preparation (i.e., winging it)
b. Failing to enjoy the moment (enthusiasm about what you are saying is critical)
c. Lacking conviction in what you have to say (if you have something to say, then say it boldly—if not, sit down!)
d. Focusing on the non-listeners in the audience instead of those who are captivated and attentive

e. Believing that shorter presentations are easier than longer ones (the exact opposite is usually true)

If you fall prey to these common mistakes, *The Top Performer's Guide to Speeches and Presentations* can make a great impact on your ability in front of a team or audience. In the next chapter, we will cover four cornerstones to a powerful presentation that will help you avoid these mistakes and give killer presentations.

Tips from the Pros

Kelly Brady (who we referred to in our introduction) is the Senior Pastor at Glen Ellyn Bible Church in Glen Ellyn, Illinois. He had this to share about his speaking experiences:

Q) What was your greatest fear starting out as a speaker?

A) My greatest fear initially was that I would have nothing of value to say.

Q) What was your worse speaking blunder?

A) When I started out I would overstate the truth, making blanket statements like "all", "never", "always", etc. I have learned since that there are very few blanket statements and people resist your ideas when you overstate them.

Q) How do you prepare for a talk?

A) I ask myself, "What do I want them to know, feel, do?" I work on the text first, identify the message of text, bridge it to make it apply to the audience, and illustrate it. I then practice delivering my sermon in real time. I sometimes go into the auditorium to practice, also.

Q) What distinguishes you as a speaker?

A) I think it is a combination of vulnerability and boldness. Those two things seem to work well together, although we don't usually think of them together.

Q) What is the #1 most important thing you can do to make a talk soar?

A) Making sure the "aha" moment happens. When truth is made accessible, digestible, and applicable, then people get inspired and want to take action.

TAKING YOUR SPEAKING TO THE NEXT LEVEL

Exercise: Qualities of great speakers

1. Write down the names of three people who you think are great speakers.
2. Name five things that their speaking styles have in common.
3. Which of these skills do you want to improve in yourself?

Suggested activity: Video evaluation

How many of you have ever taken a professional golf lesson? When you go to that pro, the first thing he or she has you do is hit a couple of balls. This way, the professional can get a sense of your baseline performance. We are asking you to do just that: Videotape yourself giving a presentation. If you can't film yourself giving an actual live presentation, then at least film yourself practicing. Dress up, use a PowerPoint (if appropriate), move and use your voice—do everything that you would do if it was real. This baseline will be used in several exercises throughout the book to help you gain insights into your strengths and challenges as a speaker. So don't procrastinate! Get out there on the course and hit a few balls!

CHAPTER 2

THE FOUR CORNERSTONES: CONVICTION, PREPARATION, DIRECTION, AND DELIVERY

Have You Ever…?

Have you ever felt like you have gotten in over your head with a speaking engagement? I was doing a presentation in Phoenix, Arizona, and a woman approached me afterwards and asked if she could recommend me to speak at something called "the million dollar roundtable." Of course I agreed, and promised to send her a tape of me speaking to use with her recommendation. I had forgotten about the encounter until she called me up and asked me to do a sample presentation in front of a panel of people. So I drove to the appointed hotel and walked into a room containing forty-five people, a U-shaped table, tons of AV equipment, and several cameras. I sat down and was told that the panel consisted of:

- Eight international speech experts/coaches from different countries
- Fifteen men over the age of sixty-five who were past presidents of the Million Dollar Roundtable (one of the insurance industry's most prestigious conferences)

- Various other experts
- The production crew

All of a sudden I realized that this was really a big deal. I gave my presentation while these people just sat and watched me. Then they sent me to a little room where I waited for some time before a person came back and congratulated me—they had chosen me to speak at their conference. Now, I still had no clue about how big this meeting was, but I figured it must be a pretty massive event given how much scrutiny I was under. Then they asked if I could be prepared to bring a lot of handouts to the events because they wanted me to be a platform speaker. "Absolutely. How many do you need?" was my response. Their answer—15,000. I was led to a mini "mock-up" of the event complete with a model of the stage, which also included all of these miniature people to show where the audience would be. I was in for a big event.

The day they flew me out to Las Vegas to do the presentation, I was feeling some major jitters. I had done a lot of speaking, but never before an audience this size. My escort took me to the green room (the room where performers relax when they're not needed onstage) and they powdered me up and walked me around to the back of the stage. Backstage was anything but warm and fuzzy; it was dark and filled with technical people trying to make sure the sound systems, microphones, computers, etc. were all in working order. So from this dark and somewhat lonely area I peeled back the curtain to take a peek. I couldn't even see the back of the room: All I saw was a sea of people, 15,000 blue blazers, white shirts and red ties, and my adrenaline started to kick up. As self-doubt began to creep in—What could I possibly have to say to these people? Do I belong here? Can I get out of this?—I remembered something: I knew what I was doing. Did I have conviction about my message? Absolutely! Did I prepare? Extensively! Did I have a direction? Clearly. And did I know how to deliver well? Positively! By mastering the four cornerstones, I knew that I could nail that presentation and get 15,000 people ready to take action on my message. With that level of confidence I was able to give a stirring and impacting presentation.

The Four Cornerstones

We have spent a large part of our careers studying what makes a great speaker. We have analyzed top speakers across several industries and come up with four things you need to have a great presentation. We call these the four cornerstones:

- Conviction
- Preparation
- Direction
- Delivery

Conviction

Great speakers have conviction about their message. They have a belief in and passion for their topic; great speakers believe that their audience *needs* to hear what they have to say. They are on a mission to impact others with what they have to share.

Let's say you have a brand new product. How do you get conviction for it? Conviction starts with believing that, first of all, your message is appropriate for the audience. You need to be able to show the audience that there's a need for your specific product or benefit. Do enough research to fully understand the product because you have to understand what it's really all about—and one of the most important things to know is what your product does better than every single one of its competitors. If you don't know why your product or message is superior, you aren't even going to believe what you're saying. How, then, could you possibly convince anyone else to believe you? Know your facts, have confidence in your position, and be ready to defend it. When it comes down to it there are three components needed to form conviction:

1. Know your topic–you have to study your topic and be an expert on it.
2. Believe what you know–your belief in your topic and points has to be 100 percent genuine.
3. Experience what you are conveying–either through

personal experience or firsthand observation you must see for yourself that it works!

For example, when I was a twenty-five-year-old I could talk theoretically about the need to save for retirement and the need to allocate your assets. However, I could only have a certain level of conviction. Once I saw others suffer by not saving and once I became older and the realities were closer than ever before, I developed much more conviction on the topic. Know it, believe it, and experience it and you will have powerful conviction.

Preparation

Great speakers prepare. They work at their presentations, and they work hard. Sometimes we look at people who have accomplished great things and attribute it only to talent, but most successful people have an incredible work ethic. For example, in the excellent book *From Good to Great* we learn the story of a man who knew the value of preparing. David Scott is a six-time winner of the Hawaiian Iron Man Athlete event, which is a grueling event that involves swimming for 2.4 miles, cycling for 112 miles and then running a 26.2-mile marathon. He's won this event six times and needless to say he did so by being in phenomenal shape. Part of the reason for his success is that he was fanatical in his preparation and training. For example, for training reasons he was on a no fat diet. For breakfast he ate cottage cheese, but he had a little ritual that he performed before eating. David Scott took every little single curdle and rinsed it off with water. The reason? He was on a no fat diet. So he was rinsing every small little particle of fat off that cottage cheese before he ate it. You might say that this guy is really weird. What we say is that David Scott knows the value and rewards of preparation. Most top performers know the value of obsessive preparation. Extraordinary golfer Tiger Woods has a personal motto of "You're never there." Lance Armstrong, seven time winner of the Tour de France, has said, "I make my practices so hard that the races seem easy." Inventor Thomas Edison defined genius as "1 percent inspiration and 99 percent perspiration," and he was right—successful people work hard, most of the time harder than anyone else is willing to do. Successful people practice and prepare.

There are many ways to prepare for a presentation. Common preparation themes include:

• Research your topic–Anytime you develop a new presentation you must make sure you have done your research. We mentioned that research is crucial in developing conviction, but it is also crucial as a preparation mechanism. If you don't spend enough time developing your content, your presentation may entertain but will fail to have the "meat" necessary to motivate your audience. A well-researched presentation will save you from potentially embarrassing situations such as presenting ideas that contradict known facts with which your audience is familiar.

- Rehearse your presentation–One of our primary philosophies is the rule of 7: We encourage participants to practice any new talk seven times before it is ever presented to an audience. The first couple of times out of the gate it will be rough. By the third and fourth times, you will start to get in the groove. By the seventh time you should be completely comfortable and confident. By practicing, you discover the rough edges and make changes to your content or to your delivery to smooth them out.

- Prepare for difficult speaking situations–There are many things that can go wrong during a talk: Crowded conference rooms, poor ventilation and lighting, technical failures, changes in time allotments, hostile participants in the audience, etc., can all interfere with an otherwise great presentation. Be ready to handle these. Check out your room in advance, have backups for any potential technical problems, be able to shift the length of your presentation at the last minute, know how to handle objections—all of these are important parts of your preparation. In general, we are in the room and ready to speak at least an hour before our presentation, which has saved our necks on a number of occasions.

- Know your audience–One of the things that we often see is speakers who fail to prepare for their specific audience. These speakers are often in for a rude awakening; you have to know your audience before you know how to motivate them. Who are they? What do they need? Why would they care about what you have to say? In order to answer these questions, we use the acronym STOP to remind us of the information you need to know in advance of your talk:
    - S – Situation: The "S" in our STOP reminder is where you do the majority of your research. You need to know what you are walking into. Things you need to know about the situation include:
        - Age, culture, and gender of your audience – Think about how relevant and relatable your stories will be to this particular group.
        - Experience and knowledge level – Review your content to make sure it is not over their heads or insulting to their intelligence.
        - Sphere of influence (i.e. who are the influential people in your audience that could impact the rest of the participants?) – Try to find out how these people feel about your topic; interview them if possible.

- Goals and Goldmines – Find out what their goals are and tap into these in your presentation; if possible, offer suggestions for how they might reach these goldmines.
- T – Time: How much time do you have to present? What types of breaks are expected? Are there any other speakers or situations that may interfere with your time frame?
- O – Objections: What are possible objections or landmines you may be walking into? Make sure that you are proactively addressing these in your talk before they object.
- P – Presentation materials: What materials do you need? How many participants will be in the session? If you have props, gifts, handouts, etc., you need to make sure that you never run short!

For example, I was recently asked to train people in Korea on coaching skills. Now, I have a sure-fire program that I do in the United States on this, but I had to review the entire presentation before going to Korea. I had to walk through my stories and delete all cultural biases or confusions. I prepared for three months before I went to Korea. I bought three different books on Korean culture, did in-depth interviews with my hosts, listened to tapes of the Korean language, and spoke to colleagues who had been to Korea. I wanted to discover cultural landmines—

where might Koreans disagree with something that a U.S. audience would automatically accept? For example, most Americans quickly accept that working on self-confidence is a positive thing to do. This was not the case with my Korean participants. In fact, I received resistance to the idea! Some participants felt like working on their confidence was too self-centered and presented the danger of appearing like they were trying to elevate themselves over their peers. To elevate oneself over peers was viewed very negatively. By knowing this I could address it proactively and we had a great discussion about how we could work on our confidence and ALSO help those around us rise with us!

Another issue that came up in my research was that Korean participants might be less comfortable with interactive exercises. Many of them prefer lecture to experiential work. By knowing this in advance I was able to increase the amount of lecture in my talk and also address the cultural difference directly by letting them know that some parts of my presentation might be outside of their comfort zone. I also discovered that the way I received a participant's business card was a potential landmine that could incite a backlash. I learned it is proper to receive the card with both hands and to study it before placing it in a place of prominence (very different than how we manhandle and write on our business cards here). By knowing the audience, I was able to give a solid presentation and avoid potential offensive or uncomfortable issues. The result? I have been invited back yearly to train for this group. Knowing your audience can save you a lot of grief and make you a much more impacting speaker. So remember to STOP and research before you present!

Here is the point: There's a lot to prepare for even if you are only giving a 30-minute talk. You have to be prepared to adapt. One of the great lessons my father taught me when I played third base in little league was to always think about what I would do if the ball came to me. I would always envision exactly how I would handle the different types of hits that could come my way. By being prepared, I wasn't a victim to ill-informed judgment that could hurt the team or cause me to lose my position …except once. That particular game, I was daydreaming when someone hit the ball almost over the third base bag. I quickly grabbed the ball and threw the runner out at first. Sounds like a great move, right? It would have been—except for the runners who were previously on first and second. If I had touched the base and thrown the ball to second or first, we would have gotten the two outs we needed. Instead, we only got one out and the runners eventually were able to score. We lost the game because I wasn't ready. It was the first and last time I failed to heed my father's advice to be prepared. Preparation is a crucial cornerstone to a great presentation and will make a huge difference.

Direction

Top performers have direction: They know where they're going to go in their presentation and they have an efficient and powerful path cleared to get there. They have the ability to be structured yet make it look like there isn't any structure to the presentation at all. They are not mechanical or stiff, but there is no doubt that underneath their voice, movements, and overall style is a solid foundation. They know exactly the impact they want to have with their presentation and they're going to get their audience there. We can form an analogy of the need for structure by looking at the automobile industry. What is the first thing that comes down the assembly line? It is the frame or the chassis—where a car has to be started, on which the rest of the vehicle has to be built. As it moves down the assembly line the last thing that goes on is the beautiful exterior body of the car.

It is the same way in a presentation. The presentation starts with a structure. There's a direction, there's an introduction, there's a time when you make a case, and a time to advance your message. The last thing you put onto that framework is your own style, like that body that comes down and encapsules the chassis. A great style distracts from the structure of the presentation and just makes it seem attractive. A driver doesn't see the chassis, only the beautiful, slick-bodied cars. Your audience should not see your structure; that is not what they are buying. However, it has to be there to hold the presentation together and ensure that it runs like a machine.

Delivery

Delivery is how it all comes out; how you present your knowledge, insights, and views to the audience (whether it be one person or one thousand). We have three primary tools for delivering a message with style: our eyes, our voice, and our body. Think of a rocket ship (shown below). If the payload is the message, the engine is the delivery of our presentation. And as we all know, the payload goes nowhere without an engine.

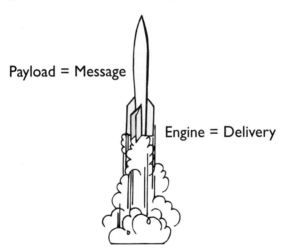

Your eyes, voice, and body movements are the external reflection of what is going on internally. If you have a high level of damaging fear, your eyes, voice, and body will show it. If you fail to master your delivery, even the best message will be discounted or at the very least you will distract the audience from the intended impact. In the next chapter we will focus on this fourth cornerstone to master the use of these powerful and essential tools.

Tips from the Pros

Tim Brown is partner and executive vice president of public relations for Richter 7, the largest locally owned advertising/PR/interactive firm in Salt Lake City. He offers these presentation tips:

Q) What was your greatest fear starting out as a speaker?

A) *Initially wondering if those I spoke to would think I was wasting their time. Wondering if the information would be valuable.*

Q) What was your worst speaking blunder?

A) *I train on creative thinking, and in one part, I have participants act like a kid again. I do this, in part, by having them spray each other with cans of silly string and throw squishy toy balls. Unfortunately, no one factored in the low-hanging chandeliers or glasses on tables in the ballroom full of 700 participants. I heard glass crashing and hoped the hotel staff wasn't close by.*

Q) How do you prepare for a talk?

A) *I first consider the audience. I figure out what they already know (so as not to insult their intelligence). I determine my key messages to them (the points I want to make, realizing they will really only remember three or four items from most presentations). I figure out the best way to present those points so it engages them (having them act things out, come to the front, answer questions, write answers to questions I'll ask, etc.). Then I put the presentation together with whatever makes sense (e.g., PowerPoint, flip charts, movie segments, dimensional pieces [balls, silly string, etc.]).*

Q) What distinguishes you as a speaker?

A) *I'm tall. Okay, that's not a big deal. I present in a conversational way so the audience and I connect sooner rather than later. I am comfortable with being witty, with fielding questions, with using movie clips, with mixing things up (once I had 550 bankers throwing frozen waffles around at each other — BANKERS!).*

Q) What is the #1 most important thing you can do to make a talk soar?

A) *Engage the audience and speak to points they can use to improve their situation. They are there to figure out what's in this presentation that will benefit them. So give them information, ideas, etc., to fulfill that.*

TAKING YOUR SPEAKING TO THE NEXT LEVEL

Exercise: The top-ten test

Rate yourself on the following ten tendencies. Please rate yourself honestly.

I start my presentations with a unique story.

Never	Rarely	Sometimes	Most times	Always

When I tell a story I end with naming the point of the story.

Never	Rarely	Sometimes	Most times	Always

I give a concise overview of what I am going to present before I present it.

Never	Rarely	Sometimes	Most times	Always

I keep my comments to a maximum of three major points.

Never	Rarely	Sometimes	Most times	Always

I give supporting evidence for each of my main points.

Never	Rarely	Sometimes	Most times	Always

I know exactly the three points I want to make before I start speaking.

Never	Rarely	Sometimes	Most times	Always

I name the benefits to my audience for acting on my three points.

Never   Rarely   Sometimes   Most times   Always

I make a specific request of my audience at the end of my presentation to move them to action.

Never   Rarely   Sometimes   Most times   Always

I briefly review my three points at the end of my presentation.

Never   Rarely   Sometimes   Most times   Always

I end my presentation with an inspirational story or by tying into my first story.

Never   Rarely   Sometimes   Most times   Always

Give yourself 5 points for your "Always" responses, 4 for "Most times," 3 for "Sometimes," 2 for "Rarely," and 1 for "Never." Now total up your scores and put the total here: _____

By the time you finish this book you will be able to rate yourself at a perfect 50 total points. In fact, you may want to take this survey again after you have practiced the material in order to see your improvement!

CHAPTER 3

PERSONAL SPEAKING TOOLS: EYES, VOICE, AND BODY

Have You Ever…?

Have you ever watched a presentation that reminded you of a bad car accident? You know the type—really painful and ugly to witness, but you just can't take your eyes off of it. A couple of years ago I had the unfortunate experience of watching a presenter go downhill quickly. The presentation was being done before a small audience. It was a team of seven and the manager had to convince them to cut their budget significantly and yet also increase results (not an easy sell for even the most experienced of presenters). The manager had hired me to observe his presentation and coach him afterwards on how he could improve for the future. There was a lot of work to be done; fortunately, I brought a large pad to take notes.

He began by telling his team that he had some news they were not going to like, but that he was confident they would rise to the challenge and overcome the obstacle. Unfortunately, his tone as he said this was anything but confident—you could immediately tell that he was fearful of their reaction. He then started a PowerPoint presentation that consisted of fifty-seven slides. Each slide was almost all text and the font size was so small on some of them that you couldn't make out the words. He talked his team through the reasons for the budget cuts, the tactics he was proposing to increase production, the potential sales figures for the next year, etc., all by reading each slide from the screen (his back was turned to us for much of the time). During the presentation he kept playing with his pen and even dropped it on a few occasions. I'm sure I was not the only person who wanted to jump up and rip it out of his hand. As he ended his monologue, he asked the group if they had any questions. Stunned looks were all he received in return. He finished up with a classic "rah-rah, we can do it" speech delivered with all the passion of a rock. It was obvious we had work to do, and the good news is that he was very open to feedback. With time and effort he became an excellent presenter in whom people could believe. You must be aware of how you come off as a speaker to establish your credibility and get results. In this chapter we will look at your credibility as a speaker—what helps it and what hurts it.

What Top Performers Know about Presentations

Do people believe you as a presenter? A fascinating UCLA personal communication study by Dr. Albert Mehrabian examined the role of verbal elements (such as word choice), voice, and visual presentation on the audience's perception of the speaker's attitude. He looked at the percentage of impact that each of these had on the audience's perceptions. Here is what he found:

Verbal = 7%

Voice = 38%

Visual = 55%

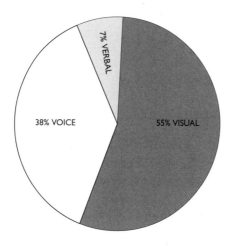

So, 93 percent of the audience's perception of your attitude—and thus the believability of your message—has less to do with the words you choose than how you say them and how you look as you're saying them. This is why top performers spend time mastering their delivery. Rookie presenters spend all of their time on their PowerPoint slides; top performers believe that the fewer slides, the better. YOU are the message, not some words on a screen.

Fear in Delivery

Let's return to the concept of damaging fear and see how it relates to the first three cornerstones and reveals itself in the delivery. Each cornerstone interfaces and relates to the others. Imagine that you are the presenter at a big meeting. What is your mindset going into the presentation? It relates to the first three cornerstones, doesn't it? How much conviction do you feel about your message? How much have you prepared? How well have you structured your talk? If you have low conviction, poor preparation, and limited direction, your condition is likely characterized by a high level of damaging fear. Your fear is there to tell you that you've set yourself up for failure!

As we have mentioned, to have some fear before a presentation is not only normal, but also actually helpful. If you are not nervous before you get up in front of a group, don't get up: Sit down, because you are not taking the presentation seriously enough. If you are not feeling the adrenaline rush that comes to a top performer, you must not care enough about your message. We need to respect our audiences, be they six people or six thousand. Not having any fear or experiencing damaging levels of fear can both kill a presentation.

So how can you tell that a presenter is suffering from fear? It shows up in the delivery via your:

- Eyes
- Voice
- Body movements

What Messages Are You Sending Your Audience?

The first place where fear shows up is in the eyes. When there's very little eye contact, or your eyes are darting around, your fear has taken over. The message you are sending your audience is, "I'm not confident in what I am sharing with you." Next, fear shows up in your voice. Perhaps you are speaking in monotone or your voice is cracking, or you may be speaking rapidly, which sends the message that "I have nothing to say so let me at least say it quickly," or "I'm not prepared." Struggling to get to your next point suggests that you have no structure or belief in your message. Finally, fear presents itself in your body movements. Nervous speakers make repetitive, predictable, and distracting movements. Certainly we encourage you to be animated and move around, but it is distracting and destructive to your message to be repetitive in your walk, gestures, etc. See the chart below to summarize our comments about a delivery going poorly.

Delivery		
Presenter Condition	**Presenter Mode**	**External Reflection**
• No conviction • No preparation • No direction	• High level of damaging fear	• Eyes—darting, floor • Voice—monotone, cracking • Body—distracting, repetitive movements

Delivery

How moved would you be by this speaker's message? How convinced would you be to buy what the speaker is selling? Obviously you will get bored, distracted, or even worse, suspicious. There is no way in the world you are going to believe what the speaker is saying.

Delivery goes well when you master the first three cornerstones. Contrast the negative image of the poor speaker with that of a speaker who has high conviction, full preparation, and a powerful direction. This person has done her homework. She has rehearsed the presentation at least seven times and has learned and tweaked after each practice session. She has a healthy level of fear because she respects her audience and sees her message as incredibly important. She wants to impact the audience and she has the confidence and conviction to do it well.

So how does a top performing presenter use his or her eyes, voice and body? He or she masters delivery by:

- Making eye contact
- Strategically using inflection and pauses
- Moving with a purpose

Making Eye Contact

What are the benefits of making eye contact with your audience? Top performers use their eyes to get buy-in from others. They also use their eyes to take energy from interested participants in the audience. Eyes are "the windows to the soul" and powerful tools in presentations. When we perform workshops, one exercise we have participants do is to stare at another person, retina to retina, for a full minute. We start the clock and every time someone laughs or breaks eye contact we restart the clock. As you can imagine, we restart the clock many times. Then we put them in groups of three and have them practice maintaining eye contact for just five seconds with each person while talking. This teaches the participants the appropriate amount of time to "visit" an audience member. We call these "focused visits." A focused visit is eye to eye, made in order to get buy-in, and only lasts for about five seconds. This level of eye contact is comfortable for most people and will create a connection and bond with the audience member. People trust people who can look at them in the eye.

Inflection and Pauses

Top performers use inflection for impact and pauses for power (for example, a pause is often appropriate at the end of a moving story). Voice inflection is used purposefully and grabs the audience's attention. While inflection sounds easy to do, most of us think we are using more than we are actually are. In our workshops, we have participants tell a story and consistently raise their voice as they speak until they reach the middle of the story. They then decrease their voice from that point on until they reach the end of their story. This is often good for a laugh—most participants sound the same across most of their story. We think we are using our voice more effectively than we really are.

Along with inflection, top performers know the power of the pause. In fact, we believe that the highest level of speaking ability is shown by the person who has learned to master the pause. Many speakers fear the pause, and they shouldn't. Despite the discomfort of not speaking when you're in front of a crowd, the pause can be dramatically powerful in bringing a point home. Pausing with a purpose says, "This is important," "This requires thought," and "This is what you need to leave with." Mastering the pause means mastering your own fear and building the ability to really grab your audience. But you have to know where to put it and you have to have the courage to use it. Pausing and silence bring people to you.

Moving with a Purpose

Have you ever seen a speaker who paces back and forth for his or her entire presentation? At first the behavior is repetitive and then it becomes predictable, and once it's predictable it becomes distracting and you have lost your audience. Speakers with repetitive and predictable movements look like caged lions pacing back and forth, yearning for freedom. Their adrenaline has gone too far and they are going to lose their audience. Even simple movements can cause problems. I was at a national sales meeting years ago where one speaker had a little habit of grabbing his earlobe. In a 20-minute speech he touched his ear thirteen times! I talked with him afterwards to give him some feedback and he had absolutely no awareness of his nervous habit. It is frightening to consider that we may have a twitch that is so automatic that we're oblivious to it. This is why videotaping yourself presenting is important.

Top performers have one rule for moving their body: move with a purpose. No movement should be performed that does not drive a point home, create energy, recapture an audience, or consciously create motivation and attention.

Repetition becomes predictable and predictability creates distraction.

The solution is moving with a purpose.

If you are going to build a house, you had better have a hammer, drill, screwdriver, and all the other necessary tools. If you are going to be a top performer, you need to master focused visits, inflection for impact and the pause for power, and finally, movement with purpose. Master these and your audience will believe you. Fail to do so and all of the pretty words and PowerPoint slides in the world will not save your presentation. These positive elements of delivery are summarized in the chart below:

Delivery		
Presenter Condition	**Presenter Mode**	**External Reflection**
• Conviction • Preparation • Direction	• Healthy Fear	• Eyes—focused visits • Voice—controlled inflection and pause • Body—movement with a purpose

Tips from the Pros

Clay Nelson is a public speaker with several decades of experience. He shared the following tips:

Q) What was your greatest fear starting out as a speaker?

A) *As a business and personal coach I've trained myself to read people, and when I am in a room full of people my senses go crazy. So starting out, my greatest fear was that I would walk out in front of a room and not remember what I was supposed to say, because my sense of what was going on in the room took me in a completely different direction. Over time, I've learned to tone down those senses when I'm speaking at a conference and still be with the people in the room, but stay on track with what I was brought there to do.*

Q) What was your worst speaking blunder?

A) *I learned a valuable lesson about making sure I don't put my microphone on before using restroom facilities; several years ago just prior to the start of a program I decided to use the restroom facilities just one last time, and my wireless restroom facilities just one last time, and my wireless microphone was not only clipped on but the power was on. My assistant, who was still in the room, realized what was happening but couldn't get into the men's restroom to tell me to turn it off. We laugh about it to this day, but I wouldn't want it to happen again!*

Q) How do you prepare for a talk?

A) I practice...practice...practice, and I make sure I know the audience I'm speaking to. Through researching the audience's industry and the latest news coming out of that industry I can personalize the message, and the need to practice speaks for itself. I thoroughly go over the PowerPoint and notes with my staff and on my own, and just prior to any big talk I go to the gym and work out. It gets my blood pumping and energy high, allowing me to make a difference and provide what I've been asked, and am expected, to give the audience.

Q) What distinguishes you as a speaker?

A) There is obviously no shortage of public speakers with great content to give their audiences, but what distinguishes me as a speaker is:

- *My knowledge of the topics I speak on.*
- *The energy I give each and every time I step on stage.*
- *My commitment to give what I have to say to everyone in the room.*
- *My ability to read the room and the people in it. I've even*

completely chucked a planned program where I was given leeway with regard to the topic I was presenting, in order to go with where the people and the energy in the room needed to go.

Q) What is the #1 most important thing you can do to make a talk soar?

A) *The most important thing for any speaker to do is to absolutely be with the participants in the room. Forget the PowerPoint behind you, forget your stack of notes and be with the room, not with your speech.*

TAKING YOUR SPEAKING TO THE NEXT LEVEL

Exercise: Using your voice

The exercise here is the voice exercise that we mentioned earlier in the chapter. It may seem silly, but we strongly encourage you to do it. Ideally you can audiotape yourself while doing it to get added feedback. What we want you to do is tell a story and incrementally increase the volume of your voice to a very loud level by the middle of it. Once you reach the middle, start decreasing the volume of your voice until you reach your original level by the end of the story. There should be about ten levels of measured difference between your start and your middle, then again between your middle and your end. Give it as much voice inflection as possible while still staying in a reasonable volume range. Part of this is how loud you can get and the other part is how quiet you can get and still be heard. So pull out the recorder and start telling your story. When you are done, answer the following questions:

1. How well did you change your voice inflection as you told your story?

2. How do you think great speakers use voice inflection?

3. When might you want to use this skill in your presentation?

If you are not satisfied with your range of inflection, keep doing the exercise until you master the skill. Great speakers use a huge range of voice when they present. Practice until you can use it when you need it.

Assignment: Review your speaker tape

Review the video of your presentation that we asked you to do in Chapter 1. Watch it with the sound off and just concentrate on your body movements. What nonverbal habits show up on your video? What movements do you make that are repetitive and thus predictable and distracting? Make a conscious effort to change these habits.

SECTION II

RIGHT BRAIN ENGAGEMENT: DON'T BE A HALF-BRAIN SPEAKER

CHAPTER 4

RELATING TO YOUR AUDIENCE THROUGH STORY

Have You Ever…?

Have you ever had people reading the paper or playing with their Blackberries or phones during one of your presentations? I was doing a presentation for a major financial services firm on a Saturday morning at 9:00 a.m. These were the firm's top producers and I think the average age had to be about fifty years old. That's the hardest, toughest audience to present to in the financial services industry, bar none. They have been incredibly successful and often doubt that anyone can tell them anything that they don't know. The person who spoke before me had been this portfolio manager who focused on graphs and charts and tax strategies, so the audience went from this complicated tax strategy piece to my presentation on how to use the power of stories to sell financial products. As I was introduced I noticed three guys in the back row. All three of them were reading *USA Today*. All in a row! They were reading before I was introduced and they continued reading as I started my presentation. I knew immediately that I needed a unique opener to catch their attention. So I started with a simple question:

How many of you in this room have ever tried to sell investments to a relative? Who has had to explain investments to your parents?

I went on to tell this story:

So here's the deal: my parents, Bob and Janet, are an interesting little couple. They're from Dayton, Kentucky, which is just south of Cincinnati, Ohio, and that's where they were born and raised. They met each other in kindergarten, they knew each other all the way through elementary school, they dated all the way through high school, and they're both from very poor, poor families.

At this point the "three amigos" are still holding their papers, but are glancing a little bit in my direction. I went on to say:

My dad received a football scholarship to Purdue and he played there for four years. Later he got drafted to the New York Bulldogs and played for six weeks until he severely separated his shoulder. He then went back to Purdue University in 1950. This is right after the war of course, and he became an assistant and head football coach at Purdue for twenty-five years. He left there and went into the administrative offices as the assistant athletic director for another twenty-three years. He was at Purdue University for forty-eight years.

The three gentlemen are now looking more at me than at their papers (people in the financial services industry often like stories related to sports; many of them are former athletes).

One day I get a phone call from my mom and she tells me that my dad is leaving Purdue. He is going to retire and they want my help with making some decisions about their finances. Of course I agree and as I am driving down I-65 to Lafayette, Indiana, I am thinking about talking to my parents about their retirement and I'm worried that they will not have enough money because he was a coach when coaches weren't making the big bucks. So I arrive and start talking to my father. Now, you have to understand my dad. My dad is your classic Big Ten coach, kind of a gruff guy. All three of us sit at the table and my parents scoot this little brochure across the table that tells me how much money we have to work with. I see the number and am pleased because they are going to be okay.

The guys in the back are now listening pretty attentively, like hunters who just spotted prey.

So I see that my parents have their money primarily in fixed income and I know that I need to get them to diversify their investments. So I start talking to my dad about equities. I talk about the DOW, the NASDAQ, I talk about international investing and I even start to sketch out the efficiency frontier. My father just looks at me and says, "I don't understand a thing you're saying." So I am sitting there feeling like a loser because I'm in financial services and I can't even talk to my parents about investing. Then it comes to me: I have to use my father's world to explain these concepts, not my own. So I remember a marketing campaign from the past where we used offense and defense to explain the need for a balance between equities and bonds in a portfolio. Here is what the conversation looked like:

My father looked at me with a little scowl, made a slight nod, and then went to talk to my mother. That is a big yes from a football coach.

At this point the three amigos were fully engaged; *USA Today* was put aside and they were into the presentation. I ended the story by asking, "How many times do you sit down and talk to clients about an investment and they just stare blankly at you?" They stayed engaged for the entire presentation.

Here is the point: It was one more time in a presentation where I saw how stories can win over the most stubborn, know-it-all, arrogant participants and get them engaged. Despite all we have studied, we are still continually amazed at how the simple technique of telling a story can gain, capture, and connect with people in the audience. So many people are hesitant to tell their stories; they have the false assumption that they do not have any interesting or worthwhile tales to tell. In fact, the first comment that many participants share is, "I don't have any stories." Because of this faulty belief they are leaving one of their most powerful tools at the door.

What Top Performers Know about Presentations

So how powerful is it to tap into the right side of the brain? Let's ask Albert Einstein. How many of you can recite Einstein's theory of relativity? Most people can't match the power of his mind and Einstein was smart enough to know this. Therefore, in a "technical" paper he wrote called "On the Effects of External Sensory Input on Time Dilation" he wrote this:

Abstract: When a man sits with a pretty girl for an hour, it seems like a minute. But let him sit on a hot stove for a minute and it's longer than any hour. That's relativity.

As the observer's reference frame is crucial to the observer's perception of the flow of time, the state of mind of the observer may be an additional factor in that perception. I therefore endeavored to study the apparent flow of time under two distinct sets of mental states.

__Method:__ I sought to acquire a hot stove and a pretty girl. Unfortunately, getting a hot stove was prohibitive, as the woman who cooks for me has forbidden me from getting anywhere near the kitchen. However, I did manage to surreptitiously obtain a 1924 Manning-Bowman and Co. chrome waffle iron, which is a reasonable equivalent of a hot stove for this experiment, as it can attain a temperature of a very high degree. Finding the pretty girl presented more of a problem, as I now live in New Jersey. I know Charlie Chaplin, having attended the opening of his 1931 film City Lights *in his company, and so I requested that he set up a meeting with his wife, the movie star Paulette Goddard, the possessor of a Shayna punim, or pretty face, of a very high degree.*

__Discussion:__ I took the train to New York City to meet with Miss Goddard at the Oyster Bar in Grand Central Terminal. She was radiant and delightful. When it felt to me as if a minute had passed, I checked my watch to discover that a full fifty-seven minutes had actually transpired, which I rounded up to one hour. Upon returning *to my home, I plugged in the waffle iron and allowed it to heat up. I then sat on it, wearing trousers and a long white shirt, untucked. When it seemed that over an hour had gone by, I stood up and checked my watch to discover that less that one second had in fact passed. To maintain unit consistency for the descriptions of the two circumstances, I rounded up to one minute, after which I called a physician.*

Conclusion: *The state of mind of the observer plays a crucial role in the perception of time.*

Taken verbatim from an article originally appearing in the *Journal of Exothermic Science and Technology* (Vol.1, No.9; 1938).

Einstein is considered by most people to have been a pretty sharp guy, and some of that monstrous intelligence is demonstrated in the fact that he knew the power of a well-told story surpassed any purely logical way of conveying information. Stories are effective because they:

- Tap into how we are wired
- Create the "aha" moment
- Generate curiosity
- Help you connect your point with your audience

Let's look at each of these in detail.

Stories Tap into How We Are Wired

Remember our receptionist story from the introduction? The right side of the brain can be either a powerful ally or enemy in getting your message across to your audience. While brain research is controversial, most scientists believe that each hemisphere specializes in different activities and functions. One particularly groundbreaking study done on the differences in the brain hemispheres was conducted in the 1960's by Roger Sperry and his colleagues. In their experiments they worked with individuals who, due to health problems, had severed the fibers that connect the right and the left hemispheres. Without these fibers (called the corpus callosum), the hemispheres could not communicate with each other—which allowed the scientists to study the functions of each side of the brain more accurately. They found some very interesting things; for instance, when an object such as a spoon was presented to the left side of the brain, the patients could name it. However, when it was presented to the right side, they could not. Also, when the spoon was presented to the right side the patient was able to show how to use it nonverbally, but could not name what it was. This and other results have caused many researchers to conclude that the left side of the brain has control over language and logic, while the right side is superior in dealing with creative elements and recognizing human emotions. While most of you do not have your corpus callosum severed, you still will respond to informational and emotional stimuli differently.

In addition to Sperry's findings, the American Speech–Language–Hearing Association cites studies showing that patients with damage to the right side of their brain have difficulty with attention and concentration, suggesting that engaging the right side of the brain is crucial for maintaining an attentive audience in your presentations. The main way we connect with the right brain is through stories, illustrations, metaphors, and analogies.

Stories are powerful because they make the unknown known; they take a difficult concept and reformat it into something the audience can understand and relate to. Take the story of my father and investments: He did not understand investing, but he did understand offense and defense. By drawing an analogy and building a brief story using the concepts he knew well, I was able to help him grasp something he did not know as well. Humans are wired this way, and the wise speaker uses stories and illustrations to keep his audience attentive and motivated.

Stories Create the "A-ha" Moment

If a story is told well it will symbolize some lesson for your audience. Ancient teachers used stories and parables that had a tremendous impact on others—think of Socrates and Aesop, masters of telling stories with a meaning buried in entertainment. A well told analogy can create the "aha" moment for your audience and gain credibility for you immediately. For example, we do much of our speaking in the world of financial services and we learned a nice analogy from a top advisor that helps people understand the need to diversify their investments. This advisor works on the fifty-fifth floor in the Sears Tower in Chicago and his clients visit him there in his office. If a client needs to be convinced of the need to diversify his or her portfolio, he takes out a pad and draws these two figures:

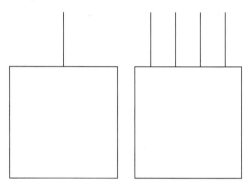

He then tells his clients that these two figures represent two elevators; one held by one cable and the other held by many cables. He asks, "If you had to ride the elevator to the 55th floor every day, which elevator would you take?" They, of course, choose the elevator with four cables. He goes on to ask, "Why's that?" to which they respond, "In case one broke." Then he says, "Right now your portfolio looks like an elevator with one cable. You are riding on that every day, and if that one cable breaks then everything is at risk. If you diversify, it is like riding the elevator with four cables." He makes the unknown known by using the familiar and most clients get it immediately and are convinced to take action.

Tips from the Pros

Brett Van Bortel is an Executive Director with Van Kampen Consulting. He speaks across the country on a variety of topics as well as works with a number of expert speakers to develop impactful content for individuals in financial services.

Q) What was your greatest fear starting out as a speaker?

A) *Everything! Were you credible? Did you seem like an impostor on the subject matter? Were you funny? Were you boring? The list goes on and on. However, the critical thing to remember is everybody starts out with difficulty. If this stopped everyone, no one would do it. Everyone is afraid at first. If they tell you differently, they are afraid to say they are afraid.*

Q) What was your worst speaking blunder?

A) *Not fully knowing my audience. Issues can grow right underneath your feet if you become complacent and assume everything is the same with this group as the previous similar group. For example, I use a joke in one presentation to financial advisors that pokes fun at a CPA's stereotypically boring personality. It's a reliable, solid laugh every time, except this one time. This group looked at me in stone silence after the joke. Then finally someone said to me, "You realize many of us are CPAs as well as financial advisors, don't you?" No, I didn't....*

Q) How do you prepare for a talk?

A) *Practice it until you are blue in the face. Prior to giving it for the first time, give the entire thing at least seven times. If it's one I haven't given in quite awhile, I will practice the opening and any other key areas in the hotel mirror prior to giving it. This helps you warm up, and shaves off any rough spots.*

Q) What distinguishes you as a speaker?

A) *I wish I had a better answer than I do. The truth to this question is not many speakers have developed a talent or trademark differentiator to a degree great enough to truly distinguish them. Most are marginally funny, or marginally expert or marginally interesting. What I have tried to hang my hat on is an effective balance between field level business expertise and humor. Then of course, there's always the hair!*

Q) What is the #1 most important thing you can do to make a talk soar?

A) *The single most important thing is to make sure they see what is in it for them. Sometimes called a WIFM (what's in it for me?). Straight up, if the audience doesn't feel that the presentation benefits them, has news for them and is extremely interesting, you will never get a chance to use all of the other skills you have developed. Only by understanding their issues and putting your message into their context, can you begin to make it soar.*

TAKING YOUR SPEAKING TO THE NEXT LEVEL

Exercise: Interesting stories

Name and describe three stories that you have heard from someone recently that you found interesting or moving.

1. _____
_____
_____
_____
_____

2. _____
_____
_____
_____
_____

3. _____
_____
_____
_____
_____

Now analyze them. What were the elements that made them interesting?

How can you use these insights in forming your own stories?

Exercise: Review your videotape

Pull out your videotape of your presentation and answer the following questions:

1. Did you tell any stories in your presentation? If you did, how clear was the message?
2. How well did you do in connecting with the right brain hemispheres of the potential audience?
3. In hindsight, how would you have started your presentation differently?

CHAPTER 5

MINING YOUR LIFE FOR STORIES

Have You Ever . . . ?

Have you ever gone on a cruise? Did you love it or hate it? For the most part I hated my cruise. For those of you who have never been on one but want to know what it is like, simply go to an all-you-can-eat buffet, have someone shake you back and forth from behind, and then sleep in the closet—you basically have had a cruise experience. However, there is one thing that redeems a cruise in my mind, and that is the excursions off the boat and doing interesting things in exciting places. One day on our cruise heading to the Cayman Islands, my oldest son Zach brought me a brochure that said, "Frolicking Family Fun" on the cover and asked me if we could do the activity. As I opened the brochure it completed the cover by saying, "Frolicking Family Fun—Go Swimming with the Stingrays." Now, I didn't think that swimming with something with the word "sting" in its name made great sense, but words like "safe" and "fun" were sprinkled throughout the brochure so I agreed to the adventure. When we arrived at Grand Cayman we boarded the smaller boat that was taking us to the lair of the stingrays. As we started getting close, our captain passed out the informed consent forms that we had to sign before they would allow us to participate. This form replaced the words "fun" and "safe" from the brochure with words like "death," "illness," "injury." In fact, death was listed several times since stingrays are poisonous if you step on their tales. Oh, and by the way, if you die it is not their fault because you were stupid enough to swim with poisonous animals that have sting in their name! Despite this, Zach and I signed the forms.

At this point, the captain of our vessel issued a challenge to the group. "The hardest part is getting one of you in the water. Once one gets in, then the rest will follow. Who is my leader in this group? Who is the brave person who will get in first?" My son Zach immediately raised his hand. As a parent my chest inflated and I looked around at the other dads thinking, "Yep, that's right, that's my boy." Then Zach did something I did not expect; he said, "My dad will do it!" My pride quickly turned to other emotions less positive, but I had no choice but to accept the challenge.

As I looked at the scary twenty or thirty stingrays swimming around the boat I had a choice; I could back down or dive in. I chose to dive in (although very carefully). After getting in the water I turned to Zach to signal him to get in. His method of diving in was to jump on my back and wrap his entire body around mine. As the stingrays surrounded us he screamed in my ear every time one touched him. But true to the captain's prediction everyone else started getting in and everyone was yelling and screaming. It was pure chaos. The scream fest lasted for several minutes. We were all out of our comfort zones and did not feel safe. However, an interesting thing happened after a few minutes: People started enjoying themselves. Eventually, we all actually did have frolicking family fun swimming with the stingrays. The point of my story is...Well, that depends on which presentation I am doing. One story can be used for several purposes. Depending on the angle you choose, you can make multiple points using the same experience. For example, I also tell this stingray story in *The Coward's Guide to Conflict*. In that book I tweaked the story and used it to make a point about fear—that "diving in" was one method of dealing with it. However, this story could be used to demonstrate many things, such as the difficulty of dealing with the unknown, how leadership requires the faith that others will follow, the point that sometimes people do the unexpected, etc. Stories can have many messages. The important thing is that you know *exactly* the point you want to make with your story before you start telling it.

What Top Performers Know about Presentations

Top performers know that stories are powerful, but they also know that the purpose of a story needs to be clear and easily applicable to the point you are making. It is all part of telling your story well (more on this later). In this chapter, we will focus on the elements of effective storytelling:

- How to tell a good story
- Key elements for using stories
- A process for pulling stories from your life

Telling a Story Well

Finding your stories is one challenge, but it is also important that you know how to share your story. What are the elements of telling a good story? Having studied effective storytellers and analyzed how they use anecdotes for amazing and impacting illustrations of their message, we have developed a three-step process that will help you build, develop, and tell interesting stories that will make your point and keep your audience engaged. The three steps are:

1. Situation: Set the stage by giving background
2. Story: Tell the story
3. Summary: Summarize and emphasize the key points or lessons learned

You always need to remember that your audience did not experience what you experienced—think about what type of background information someone would need who has no clue what you are talking about. What do they need to understand in order to follow the story? What supplementary information is necessary for them to fully get the point of your story?

The level of detail throughout your story is very important. Too much detail will bore your audience, while too little will confuse them and limit the impact of your story. Your illustration needs to flow, and in telling a story, timing is everything. That is why you want to practice it many times before going live with the illustration.

Three Key Elements to Using Stories

There are three main things you need to ask yourself about your stories:

- What is the purpose of your stories?
- Where do you use them?
- How do you develop them?

What Is the Purpose?

The overall purpose of using stories is to connect with your audience: You want to engage both the left and right hemispheres of their brains in order to motivate them to action. However, you should know the purpose of each story. As we mentioned earlier, what point are you trying to make? What is the take-away message of your story? What do you want the audience to think of when they remember your story? These questions are important to ask yourself, because a story without a purpose places you back down in the realm of an entertaining speaker.

Where Do You Use Them?

There are three main times to use a story. The first is when starting your talk. We call this the unique opener (more on that in future sections). By starting off your presentation with a story, you immediately grab the attention of your audience and put them into a receptive stance to hear your message. The second time to use a story is when you want to fully connect with them around a particular point. Stories have the power to make the complex understandable. Take simple metaphors like:

- The grass is always greener on the other side
- A stitch in time saves nine
- He's a loose cannon

We immediately get the point of these and are connected with the message of the person using the metaphor. The third time to pull in a story is when you need to simply energize the audience. People can only handle so many facts, and the attention span of the population is only diminishing. Stories bring your audience back to your message.

Developing stories may be easier than you think; we will show you a process for mining your life for good stories.

Mining Your Life

To understand and effectively use events from your own life, start cataloging things that have happened in your past and find lessons from those experiences. We will briefly describe that process here, then have you do it in the exercise section in this chapter. First, catalog interesting or dramatic things you have experienced. This includes hobbies, accomplishments and interesting situations you have encountered throughout your entire life. Second, write down one or two things that you learned from those experiences. What meaning did these experiences have for your life? What "aha" moments have you gone through? Third, tie the lessons into possible themes of your presentation. This three-step formula has proven effective in hundreds of workshops to pull stories from even the most doubting of participants. Participants who initially greeted this exercise with "I have no stories" later turned out to have very intriguing things to share.

Some examples include participants who had great accomplishments such as being an Olympian champion, marathon runner, or top gun fighter pilot. Others had intriguing hobbies like collecting high-end comic books, participating in old west gun shows and rare stamp collecting. Still others had dramatic life events to share such as saving the life of another person, near-death experiences, and touching volunteer work. Because you are so familiar with your life you may miss the fact that your experiences, hobbies, and accomplishments are fresh and new to others. Remember what is mundane to you may be magnificent to others. Don't worry if you still think you do not have any interesting stories because in the exercise section we will ask you additional questions that will help generate ideas and pull gems out from your past.

Once you have mined your life for a special story, create and develop it using the three key elements to using stories that we established earlier:

Creating Your Stories

1. Mine your life for personal stories
2. Look for unique or dramatic experiences that people might find interesting
3. Create your illustration
   - Situation—set up the background for your story
   - Story—tell the story with select detail
   - Summarize—reinforce the key point about the lesson learned which leads to your topic
3. Rehearse it! Know it! Nail it!

Tips from the Pros

John Baldoni is a leadership and communications consultant/speaker and is the author of six books on leadership, including his newest title, *How Great Leaders Get Great Results*. John shares these words of wisdom:

Q) What was your greatest fear starting out as a speaker?
A) Not knowing my material. But as they say, practice, practice, practice.

Q) What was your worst speaking blunder?

A) *Spilling my water glass on stage and watching the water drip perilously close to a power cord. Fortunately there was no damage, but it was not a proud moment.*

Q) How do you prepare for a talk?

A) *I find out all I can about my audience and relate my speaking points to their experience. It's not hard to do, but it makes a big difference in relating content to reality.*

Q) What distinguishes you as a speaker?

A) *I would like to be considered a good storyteller who provides excellent content that provokes thinking and ultimately action.*

Q) What is the #1 most important thing you can do to make a talk soar?

A) *Create engagement with the audience immediately. How? Do what trainers do: give them something to do immediately. Pose a question. Field responses.*

TAKING YOUR SPEAKING TO THE NEXT LEVEL

Exercise: Mine your life worksheet: a three-step process

Now is the time to develop your stories. Use the below worksheet to write down interesting experiences, accomplishments, and hobbies you have had, then relate the experiences to what you learned. Finally, look for possible

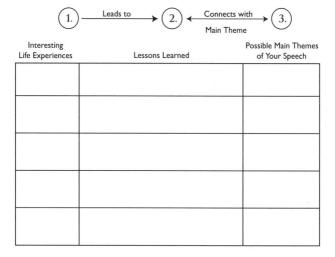

Mine-Your-Life Worksheet

themes in the story that could go with your speech.

Complete this form and try to unearth at least five

potential stories. If you are having difficulties discovering interesting life experiences, use the following questions to generate ideas:

1. What is something unusual about you that few people know?
2. What is your greatest accomplishment?
3. What was your most embarrassing moment?
4. Who was the most interesting person you ever worked with and what stories could you share about this person?
5. What story do you tell friends that makes them laugh?
6. What story did your parents always share about you growing up?
7. Think about a vacation you went on that was fun or meaningful. What made it special?
8. What do you want people to say about you at your eulogy? What stories would you like them to share?
9. What failure in your life led you to grow smarter or stronger?
10. Go through an old photo album—what memories do the pictures evoke?

Pick some experiences that popped up from these questions and finish the worksheet.

SECTION III

PRESENTATION MAPPING: FINDING YOUR WAY THROUGH A PRESENTATION

CHAPTER 6

INTRODUCING YOUR IDEA, MAKING A CASE, AND ADVANCING YOUR MESSAGE

Have You Ever . . . ?

Have you ever had your son or daughter come to you at the last minute with a school project due the next day? This can be a frustrating situation, but also an opportunity to teach your child some good lessons. At 9 p.m. one Sunday night, my 15-year old son came to me and said he had a book report on the Secret Service due the next day. After the usual parental lecture on procrastination, he and I started to problem-solve the challenge. I saw this as a chance to use some elements of presentation mapping, figuring that if it worked for corporate presentations, it should work for a book report.

After asking my son a few questions, we were able to pinpoint the top three things he wanted to say about the Secret Service. We then moved to the benefits: What did these three points mean to the reader or audience? Why should they care? How would they benefit from this information? We then called one of my buddies—who used to work for Ronald Reagan—and got a unique killer story from behind the scenes. Of course, this became my son's unique opener. I had him practice telling the story and stating his ideas concisely. He went to school on Monday and came back that evening with an "A" on his report. He beamed as he talked about how his teacher wanted to know where he got his structure so that she could share it with others. The point? If a 15-year-old boy can learn presentation mapping and get an "A," then there is hope for all of us adults.

Presentation Mapping

What if we told you that you needed to go from Chicago, Illinois, to Santa Fe, New Mexico, but that you could not use a map to help you in any way? How would you feel? Compare that feeling to the experience you would have if you went online and got a step-by-step map that spelled out where you were going? How would you feel in comparison? It is the same way with your audience. They will not feel comfortable enough to listen to you until you give them an idea of where you are going. Audiences instinctively want predictability. If they feel you are just wandering in a presentation without any direction or likely destination they will tune you out.

For that reason, we have developed a process for establishing a strong structure to your presentation that we call "presentation mapping." You have probably been taught by other books and programs that every presentation has an opening, a middle, and an end, right? We deal with these elements a little differently. We call the process "presentation mapping" because it does what any good map will do: gets us from point A to point B. If you have a good map to your presentation, you will likely reach the desired destination of motivating your audience to action. Without a map, you will probably get lost!

Presentation Mapping

These are the three elements we use to describe a presentation:

Introducing your idea.

The introduction is when you connect with the audience. You need to state the reason you are there and name your topic. Basically, you talk about what you are going to talk about.

Making the case.

Once you have connected well with the audience, you need to make your case. Here, make your main points and help the audience realize why they should care about what you have to say.

Advancing the message.

The final component is advancing the message. This is where you move your audience to next steps or action, a change in mindsets or behavior.

Introducing Your Idea

After intensively researching the techniques of top storytellers, we have developed a formula for forming a killer introduction: USC. These three components make a successful introduction every time. The U stands for unique opener. It's the first thing we start with, something unique, something different. It's definitely right brain. The S stands for clearly stating what we're going to talk about here today—tell the audience the purpose of the session. The C stands for giving the audience a concise overview. Let's cover each of these in detail.

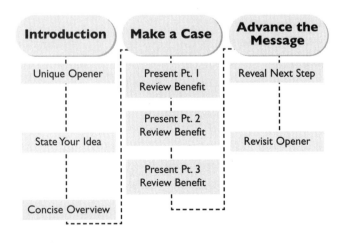

The Unique Opener

The unique opener is how you should start your presentation. We define it as an opening illustration or a personal story that is designed to demonstrate one clear message of the presentation in a dramatic or interesting way. The unique opener leads to the topic of your talk. It is the crucial first impression: Are you funny? Are you knowledgeable? Do you have something to offer? Are you able to move me? These are questions that your audience will be asking themselves as you walk up on stage or begin speaking at a meeting.

The Purpose of Your Opener

What are we trying to do when we open a presentation? Grab attention! In workshops we start many of our stories with a question; our group has done training with improvisation comedians and master speakers, and some of them refer to this as the "Leno Technique." If you watch Jay Leno on The Tonight Show, he often starts his monologue with a question before he goes on to tell his story. Questions grab people's attention, especially if it is an unusual question. Unusual questions or questions that people can relate to are a great way to start your presentation. You are showing the audience right off the bat that you will be interesting and are worth their attention.

Here's the point on this. We are trying to grab our audiences' attention, but keeping with the theme of this book, we are not just trying to grab the attention of the left side of their brain with facts and figures; and in fact, that could make the whole brain tune out. Stories engage both the left and right sides of the brain. You will only get about 30–90 seconds to engage your audience, so you do not want to waste that time with dry information. Use powerful stories to grab them emotionally and pull them in right away.

The final characteristic of a great unique opener is that it establishes your credibility. You demonstrate immediately that you are a confident and experienced speaker who knows how to relate to the audience. You are an interesting human being who has intriguing things to say. In general, the unique opener lets your audience know that you are both entertaining and knowledgeable enough to be worth listening to.

In summary, unique openers:
• Engage the right brain
• Gain attention
• Establish credibility
Unique openers are not:
• A reciting of name, rank and serial number
• One minute thank-you's
• Apologetic

We have seen a number of speakers get on stage only to embarrass themselves immediately by spending five minutes doing one of the above. Speakers who start with a monologue of facts about their background and life will either bore the audience immediately or be quickly pegged as arrogant and self-involved. Ideally, you will have someone introduce you with a brief and powerful synopsis of your background and expertise. In general, you should have this introduction written out in bullet points (for those of you speaking to audiences who don't know you) to make sure your host hits the most important points in your background—and only the most important points.

The opposite-but-equally-offensive-as the arrogant speaker is the presenter who gets up and apologizes for taking the audience's time or spends the first minute thanking the group for having him or her speak. This speaker may appear to lack confidence. Thanking the audience may sound like a good thing to do, but overdoing your gratitude sends the message to the audience that you really don't deserve to be up in front of them.

Clearly State Your Message

The "S" in the USC formula stands for stating your message. For your introduction to be effective, you must tell a story that has something to do with the topic of your presentation—you could have the funniest story in the history of mankind, but if it is unrelated to your topic you have only managed to distract your audience from your message. The takeaway from the story has to be clear: you've got to make it dramatic and engaging, but not at the sake of clarity. Practice your story and be able to clearly state the main point. Timing is crucial, and perfect timing only comes with repetition and tweaking. Spend as much time as needed to develop your introduction, as it can make or break your presentation.

One other little quick technique is the power of the pause we've mentioned. When you start your introduction with a question, make sure you pause after asking it. The pause causes people to stop and actually think about what you asked. You are creating an immediate, emotional bond between yourself and your audience in some area of commonality to which you can both relate. Just asking a simple question gets them thinking and opens an emotional rapport.

Concise Overview

The third point in our USC acronym stands for concise: at this point in your message, give a concise overview of what you plan to cover. It is important that you do not ramble in your introduction—imagine the speaker who tells a funny or interesting story, states how it relates to the topic at hand, then goes on to over-explain the message, pull in irrelevant information, and become horribly long-winded. That speaker just took the audience from being excited for to dreading the rest of the presentation. When you give your concise overview, simply address the three points you are going to make in your presentation. Trust that your audience is intelligent and capable and does not need you to hold their hand or repeat your message five times in a row, but tell them where you are going before you go there. When you tell your audience where they will be going, they can always figure out where you are at in your presentation which gives them a sense of partnership with you in the experience.

Making the Case

Your introduction began with a unique opener, then stated the main idea of your story and gave a concise overview of what you are going to talk about; now it is time to make the case. When you make the case in a presentation, you talk about three things: not four, not seven, but three. There is a power to three things. Sermons traditionally make three points, mainly because humans have a difficult time truly remembering any more than three major points in a presentation. Many rookie presenters think that the more information, the better. They could not be more wrong.

The Power of Three

For some strange reason there is power in threes. Think of all the iconic threes that we know:

- The Three Musketeers
- The Three Wise Men
- The Three Bears
- "Three Blind Mice"
- *My Three Sons*
- Three Dog Night
- *Three's Company*
- *The Three Stooges*
- *The Three Amigos*

There is some strange magic to groups of three, so when you make your case you want to think about the three most important things you can say about your topic. If you are going to talk about the future of your company or department, what are the three points you want people to remember when they walk out of your presentation? If you are selling a product, what are the three main features of it?

There is space on your presentation mapping worksheet for making your three points as well as the supporting information for them. If the USC formula in the introduction was meant to engage the right brain, then this is where you engage the left brain. Making the case is where you share the information that your audience needs to make a decision or change a behavior. See the chart below to help put this concept in perspective.

Presentation Mapping

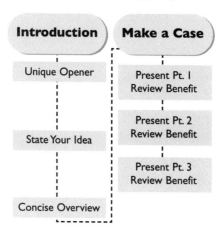

Soon we will show you a technique for creating your best three points in order to make your case in the most powerful way possible. But first, notice in the above figure that your points should be separated into features and benefits.

Features and Benefits

Once you figure out the three most crucial things about what you are presenting, you also need to communicate the benefits of these three things for the audience. You need to help them see why they should care. People don't buy features, they buy benefits; and when you're getting ready to close out your sale or presentation, the last three things they need to hear from you are three quick, solid benefits. The benefit statement is not a whole new presentation, but a concise statement of the benefits of embracing your message.

Briefly review each feature and the matching benefit. Make sure that you do all three! It is also important to have a fluid segue from features to benefits. We have found this simple statement to work well for this purpose: *"So what does this mean to you?"*

It's simple, and yet it represents the perspective of your audience. They want to know how your message applies to them—honestly, they aren't really interested in anything else you have to say.

Developing Your Three Points with Storyboarding

It is important to have a method for building the three main points you want to share in your presentation. The process we use is called storyboarding. We explain this process in detail in our book, *Coaching the Sale* so if you have read that book this will be familiar to you. If you have not read *Coaching the Sale* then storyboarding is a way to organize your thoughts. It can be used for a variety of tasks, but is especially relevant for anyone needing to prepare a presentation. It equips you to move from brainstorming to structure in a few easy steps.

In order to storyboard, all you need are sticky notes and a thick felt pen (so that you can easily read your sticky notes from a distance). Use the following steps to storyboarding your presentation:

- Identify
- Cluster
- Label

Identify

The first step is to brainstorm without judgment or doubt. To be effective, you simply need to brainstorm all of the possible things that you could say in your presentation. What are all of the points that you would like to make? As you brainstorm about these things, write each idea down on its own sticky note and plaster it to your wall or desk. Write down as many ideas as you can think of without concern for replication, plausibility or any other concern that could block a free-flowing mind. Write down ideas until you have exhausted all possibilities. So let's imagine that you are in charge of doing a presentation on increasing effective team-work in the organization. After spending fifteen minutes brainstorming you might have a wall covered with sticky notes that looks like this:

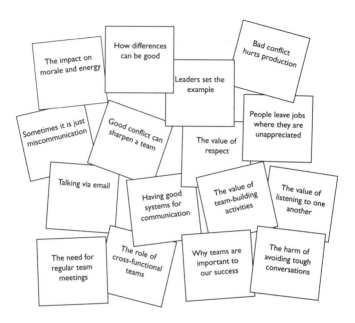

At this point you have the bare-bones of a presentation, but it is scattered and unorganized. It's time to move to the second step in the storyboarding process, clustering.

Cluster

Start moving your sticky notes around, putting similar themes together. Which ideas seem to flow with each other? Move them around, then step back and look at them; repeat this until you are sure you have clustered effectively. For our purposes you want to create three clusters. Any sticky note that does not fit into the best three clusters should be seen as detracting from your message and thrown away. You can also remove any repetitive notes or anything that does not add value to your message. Finally, feel free to add any ideas that are missing to your categories. So if we take our effective teamwork presentation ideas and cluster them, we might come up with the following clusters:

The impact on morale and energy	How differences can be good	Having good systems for communication	The value of team-building activities
Bad conflict hurts production	Sometimes it is just miscommunication	The value of listening to one another	Talking via email
The harm of avoiding tough conversations	The value of respect	The role of cross-functional teams	Leaders set the example
People leave jobs where they are unappreciated	Good conflict can sharpen a team	The need for regular team meetings	

Once you have clustered, move on to the next storyboarding step.

Label

As you review your three clusters of notes, ask yourself, "What theme brings each cluster together?" Write these category names on another sticky note in a different color and place them above their group. You could label our example as follows:

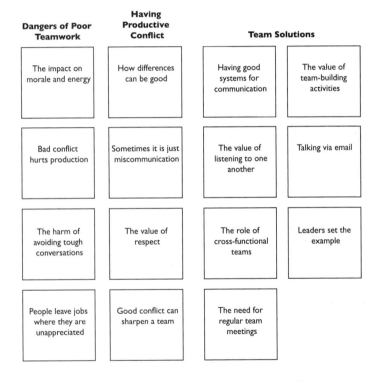

You have now built your three points and have all the necessary supporting information. As you give your concise overview of your presentation, you could say something along the lines of:

"There are three things I want to talk about today. They are: the dangers of poor teamwork, the importance of productive conflict, and solutions to take our teamwork to the next level."

As you go through your presentation, add meat to the bones by sharing the supporting information as you walk through each of the three points. You would also make sure the audience heard the benefits of embracing each of your three points and taking action on them.

The storyboarding process is fairly simple, but it manages to take complex ideas and too much information and turn it into a cohesive and impactful message. It is a straightforward process that will dramatically decrease the time you put into developing a presentation. When we trained people on presentations before we developed this storyboarding technique, it took several hours to develop a practice talk. With storyboarding, this time is cut at least in half.

Advancing Your Message

After you have done your introduction and made your case, it is time to advance your message (we sometimes refer to this as advancing the cause or the sale). This section is pretty simplistic and can be accomplished with the following statement. We encourage you to memorize it and use it often: *If you like what you saw here today, this is what you need to do to get started.* Then you simply give them the action steps. Tell them specifically what you want them to do next and how they can buy/accomplish everything you talked about in your presentation.

The Perfect Ten

If you look at our final version of the Presentation Mapping Workshop, you will see that there are ten parts to your presentation.

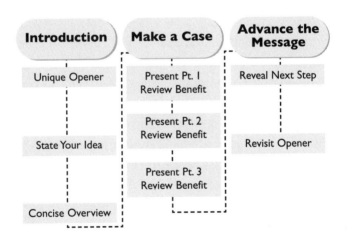

In the Introduction

Part 1: U – Start your presentation with a unique opener

Part 2: S – State the main point of your opening story

Part 3: C – Concisely give an overview of your presentation

In Making the Case

Part 4: Share your first point with supporting comments and facts.

Part 5: Share your second point with supporting comments and facts.

Part 6: Share your third point with supporting comments and facts.

Part 7: Review the benefits of them taking action on each of your three points.

In Advancing Your Message

Part 8: Revisit your key points to remind them briefly of what you told them.

Part 9: Reveal next steps – ask them to take a specific action on your ideas.

Part 10: Renew and inspire them by ending with a story (either relating back to your unique opener or adding another powerful story at the end).

These are the ten things you need to put in your presentation to make it perfect. When these simple elements are well played, you will make the impact that you are trying to make.

Heart–Head–Heart

We are sure that by now you've noticed our belief that addressing the whole brain is the most effective thing you can do as a speaker. If you look closely at The Perfect 10, you will see how they dance back and forth between the brain hemispheres. Start with the unique opener that primarily hits the right side of the brain, then move to features and benefits, which are more logical and left-brain focused. End with action, and in the ideal presentation return to the unique opener in order to leave the audience on an inspirational note (hitting the right side again). When you handle a presentation in this way you become an equipper, not just a convincer. Many speakers (or salespeople for that matter) spend great energy trying to convince their audience of their message. When a presentation is done well you have not merely convinced, but equipped your audience to practice a new skill, embrace a new idea, or change their behavior to better their life.

Tips from the Pros

Erika Oliver is a consultant, trainer, and author of *Three Good Things: Happiness, Everyday, No Matter What*. She answered our speaker questions like this:

Q) What was your greatest fear starting out as a speaker?
A) I was afraid that I would forget what I wanted to say and trip over my words. I feared not sounding intelligent.

Q) What was your worst speaking blunder?

A) *I showed up one hour late to a group of seventy-five physicians because I took a wrong turn on the highway and didn't notice for almost an hour! No matter what I said, I couldn't gain their respect after that blunder.*

Q) How do you prepare for a talk?

A) *Background research on the organization or group, storyboarding the talk, sometimes preparing a PowerPoint even if I'm not going to use it—it provides me with a visual—then rehearsing (mostly in my head), then forgetting it and being open to what the audience needs.*

Q) What distinguishes you as a speaker?

A) *Authenticity. I work hard to listen and connect and make the presentation meaningful for the audience, not for me.*

Q) What is the #1 most important thing you can do to make a talk soar?

A) *If I am confident and excited, that positive energy is picked up by the group. Equipment failure, bad attendance, background noise, and bad weather won't make a dent if I am convinced that where I am and what I am saying is the most important thing in the world.*

TAKING YOUR SPEAKING TO THE NEXT LEVEL

Exercise: Storyboarding

Think about a topic which you need to present and put it through the storyboarding process. Do the following steps:

Brainstorm: Without judgment or any screening of your ideas, brainstorm all of the different things you could say in your presentation. Put each down on a sticky note and plaster them to the wall.

Cluster: When all your ideas are exhausted, start clustering similar themes together until you are satisfied with the themes. Create no more than three main categories. Discard any sticky notes or ideas that do not flow with these three. Add any additional ideas that you think of once the categories are separated.

Label: Label your three categories, putting the category name above the group of sticky notes. You have now created your three main topics and have the supporting evidence to back them up. List them here:

CHAPTER 7

WHOLE BRAIN SPEAKING: BRINGING IT ALL TOGETHER

Have You Ever…?

Have you ever done a talk that some people loved and some people hated? I was one of the speakers at my high school graduation. However, before speaking at the ceremony, I had to do my speech before a committee made up of about six teachers at the school. In a cold and sterile classroom I stood up and gave the most moving speech I could deliver at that young age. As I ended my presentation with a challenge to take responsibility for our future, I paused to look at my audience. There was a clear divide. On one side of the room were several teachers frowning and taking notes. I found out later that they were dissatisfied with the structure of my talk and wanted me to make some major structural changes before I stood up in front of my classmates. I don't remember which teachers they were, but I do remember that they were the more logical and analytical types. If I just looked at them, I would probably have thought I did a lousy presentation. Fortunately, the other teachers were wiping tears from their eyes. My talk had moved them emotionally and they were touched by my message. One of these teachers was my favorite at school because she was a person of great passion and heart. My speech had passion, and she felt it. Here is the point: I had a good right brain talk, but didn't bring it all together to satisfy my left-brain listeners. By the time I presented at graduation, the talk was balanced. When you bring your talk together in this way you entice both the head and heart and this is what motivates people to change.

What Top Performers Know about Presentations

So what do top performers know about presentations? They know you need to prepare. They know you need to learn from each and every talk that you do. They know that, to do a killer presentation, you must talk to the head and to the heart. Throughout this book we have demonstrated ways for you to tap into both the right and left brain hemispheres in order to be a whole brain speaker. In this last chapter, we will present a few final thoughts to help you bring it all together.

Three-Step Process for Mastering a Talk

Let's imagine that you have created a masterful unique opening, are very clear on your message, and are able to concisely state what your presentation is about. You have storyboarded your presentation and discovered your three main points, as well as the best ways to elaborate on these features with supporting information, and are able to point out the benefits of each to your audience. You also know exactly what action you want to request from your audience and are prepared to make that request with confidence, then end your presentation on an inspiring note. Now you need to practice before you get in front of a live audience. Here are three simple steps for preparing to deliver your presentation:

1. Read your script
2. Read your script in acting position
3. Present without notes

This process mirrors how actors learn their lines. It is the actual process that a Bruce Willis, a Natalie Portman, or a Kevin Spacey would use. The first thing actors do is sit down and literally read the script through over and over again. The next step is reading the script in the actual position assumed while the lines are being spoken. Finally, the script is ditched. It is a simple three-step process: read it, read it in position, recite it without reading.

Using this same process as a speaker will build your confidence and help you master the timing of your presentation.

A Final Thought…

Have you ever gotten stronger by facing something that was difficult? When I was a little kid I had a hobby—like

I bet most of you did—and my little hobby was collecting bugs and insects. I used to love to collect any crawly thing. We would catch these critters and mount them on display. I had boxes of these things. I kept a "bug journal" and every time I collected one, I would check it off. I eventually started focusing on moths and I wanted to get every single species caught and mounted. I had most of them, but there was one I never could catch: a Cercropia moth. It's an incredibly huge big brown moth and I just never found one. So about a year ago I'm watching the Discovery Channel on TV with my kids, and lo and behold, they were showing a special about the Cercropia moth. The special showed the moth coming out of a cocoon on a time-lapsed camera. They showed the moth inside the cocoon and recorded how it bites through the cocoon to free itself. It chews the cocoon, spits it out, and then chews a little bit more. Finally a big hole opens up and its huge wing comes out. Then another wing pops out. Finally this gross and slimy creature comes out and within a half an hour it turns into this big, brown, beautiful moth.

Now, at the same time they showed this successful emergence they were also recording another cocoon. In order to speed up the process, they got a knife and cut the cocoon open. They took out the moth and put it on the table. But do you know what happened when they cut the cocoon? Every time they interfered with the process of the moth fighting and chewing its way out of the cocoon, the moth died. Every time. Here is the point—the moth gets its strength from the struggle. It needs to struggle to free itself from the cocoon or it does not develop the strength necessary to survive.

To be a top performer in presenting, you have to get your hands dirty with this material. You have to wrestle with it and chew on it and face the challenge head on. If you try to avoid the struggle you will also avoid becoming the best speaker you can be. The only way you'll be a stronger presenter is to fight through some of these things, make mistakes, and learn from them. It can be a struggle to find your right structure, a challenge to pick your brain for the right stories. Oh, sure, we could just hand you a great presentation, but if we did it would be the same as those scientists cutting the cocoon for the moth. Without the struggle, you will not become a top performer. And when you do, you will have your one shining moment. If you've done the work, you will make that moment shine. You will impact. You will motivate. And you will be a top performer.

Tips from the Pros

Karla Robertson is the founder and president of Shifting Gears. She speaks on the topics of leadership, breaking barriers to success, and developing your influence to drive results. She has worked with top companies in the mortgage industry. She shares the following thoughts with us:

Q) What was your greatest fear starting out as a speaker?

A) *Drawing a Blank: My greatest fear when I started speaking in front of people was that I would forget what I wanted to say or that people would be bored. Even worse, someone out there might know more than I on my topic and "expose" me via a question I didn't know the answer to. I got over that when I realized you only have to say, "Great question, I don't know the answer but give me your name afterward and I promise to get back to you." The key is to really speak about topics you know intimately.*

Q) What was your worst speaking blunder?

A) *Did I Really Say That? In my early years in sales, I was answering a question from this man who I could clearly see was missing his right arm and I was determined not to stare or make a big deal about his missing arm if we spoke. We did have a couple of exchanges, and then he asked me if he should pay three points to get a lower rate on his mortgage. Part of my answer included that the number of points he was intending to pay to get a low rate on his mortgage was going to "cost him an arm and a leg!" The room went silent. Lesson: Be aware of metaphoric phrases. You never know when they're going to bite you. So, how did I get out of this? Well, actually he let me off the hook by saying, "And I can't afford that, can I!" He was a great sport.*

Q) How do you prepare for a talk?

A) *Even the Pros Practice: Three things here: Know your topic cold. Practice, Practice, Practice. And I mean out loud. Many people only go over speeches in their heads. Or they just wing it. First, make an outline. Do NOT write out your whole speech. Second, make sure you get comfortable with what you're going to say so it sounds like you're just having a conversation with the audience. Third, have fun! Audiences love speakers who are enthusiastic and into their topic and most importantly, make it real.*

Q) What distinguishes you as a speaker?

A) *As a speaker, what distinguishes me is that I'm not afraid of putting emotion into what I have to say and allowing the audience to feel what I'm feeling. Also, since humor is a big part of who I am, I weave that into my presentations based on the vibe I get from the audience. I find that starting out with something funny that is usually aimed at myself and/or relevant to the audience gets things started off well and puts me more at ease. Physiologically, the act of laughing does release pent-up stress and muscle tenseness. Try it!*

Q) What is the #1 most important thing you can do to make a talk soar?

A) *Make your point: I know this sounds obvious but I've heard speakers who don't. Create a speech that builds on itself and doesn't wander. Your presentation should be tight, be well-*

paced, and give everyone something to walk away with at the end. Give them something powerful to chew on as your ending. They will remember you for this. Most of all, if you promise that people will walk away with something specific...make sure you deliver it!

TAKING YOUR SPEAKING TO THE NEXT LEVEL

Exercise: Pulling together your previous work

Go over all of your previous exercises and create a solid outline for your talk. If it helps you, write it out word-for-word, then practice it at least seven times.

Assignment: Videotape yourself again

Now that you know how to give a killer presentation, videotape yourself again. Compare this tape with your old tape and record the following:

I have improved in the following three areas:

1.
2.
3.

I want to continue to improve in the following three areas:

1.
2.
3.

Exercise: Final exercise

Practice! Now is the time to put the book aside (assuming you have done all the exercises!) and go out to practice your message. You will hit bumps in the road and you will make mistakes, but if you learn from each bump you will grow and strengthen to be a top performer in giving presentations!

INDEX

P

ABOUT THE
AUTHORS

Tim Ursiny, PhD

Tim Ursiny, PhD, CBC, RCC is the CEO of Advantage Coaching & Training (www.advantagecoaching.com). He is a coach/trainer specializing in helping people reach peak performance, great relationships, and personal happiness. Dr. Tim regularly speaks for Fortune 500 companies wanting workshops that are practical yet entertaining. He also coaches CEOs, executives, sales professionals, and others on a variety of subjects related to performance and life satisfaction. Dr. Tim's previous books include *The Confidence Plan: How to Build a Stronger You*, *The Coach's Handbook*, and *The Coward's Guide to Conflict*, which is currently in its third printing and has been translated into several foreign languages. He is currently writing a series of books called *Top Performers Guides* around such topics as change, conflict, and attitude.

He lives in Wheaton, Illinois, with his wife, Marla, and his three sons, Zach, Colton, and Vance. Dr. Tim can be reached at Drtim@advantagecoaching.com.

Gary DeMoss

Gary DeMoss is the director of Van Kampen Consulting,

which provides communication and relationship-skills training to financial advisors. Gary has been with Van Kampen for twenty-four years. He began his career with the company by starting and directing their national sales. He was later named director of marketing and in 1998 started Van Kampen Consulting. Gary is a keynote speaker, seminar leader, and consultant to advisors who want to build their affluent client base, and he was recently selected as a platform speaker at the 2003 Million Dollar Round Table conference.

He is the coauthor of the book *The Financial Professional's Guide to Persuading 1 or 1,000*, which helps advisors learn the science and art of delivering more powerful client presentations both one-on-one and in group settings.

Prior to joining Van Kampen, Gary was with Procter & Gamble in sales management. He has a BS in business from Miami University in Oxford, Ohio.

You can reach Gary at demossg@vankampen.com.

Jim Morel

Jim Morel is the founder/chairman and CEO of Jam Consulting Group, Inc., a sales and management consulting firm. In addition to his work as an executive sales coach and consultant, Jim is a sought-after keynote speaker. Prior to founding JAM Consulting Group, Inc., he worked for thirty years in financial services in several areas, including senior management as president of a broker dealer company, commissioned sales, and international and national sales management. Over the years, Jim has successfully rebuilt and re-energized hundreds of sales teams struggling at one time or another.

Jim holds undergraduate and graduate degrees in education, psychology, and science from Purdue University in Lafayette, Indiana. He is on numerous advisory boards and is involved with many nonprofit organizations. Jim lives in St. Charles, Illinois, with his wife, Sherry. He has three children, Tom, Kaleen, and Marques, along with six grandchildren.

You can reach Jim at moreljam@aol.com.